AW WITH WORDS

Young Writers' 16th Annual Poetry Competition

It is feeling and force of imagination that make us eloquent.

How can I not dream while writing? The blank page gives a right to dream.

East & West Sussex

Edited by Michelle Afford

 Young **Writers**

First published in Great Britain in 2007 by:
Young Writers
Remus House
Coltsfoot Drive
Peterborough
PE2 9JX
Telephone: 01733 890066
Website: www.youngwriters.co.uk

SB ISBN 978-1 84602 833 5

Foreword

This year, the Young Writers' *Away With Words* competition proudly presents a showcase of the best poetic talent selected from thousands of up-and-coming writers nationwide.

Young Writers was established in 1991 to promote the reading and writing of poetry within schools and to the young of today. Our books nurture and inspire confidence in the ability of young writers and provide a snapshot of poems written in schools and at home by budding poets of the future.

The thought, effort, imagination and hard work put into each poem impressed us all and the task of selecting poems was a difficult but nevertheless enjoyable experience.

We hope you are as pleased as we are with the final selection and that you and your family continue to be entertained with *Away With Words East & West Sussex* for many years to come.

Contents

Patcham House School, Brighton

Rydon Community College, Storrington

St Philip Howard Catholic High School, Barnham

Uckfield Community Technology College, Uckfield

The Poems

Life!

Battles the sea; fierce, power proud
Gallant crest as mounted steed rises in vain -
    crashing, crying loud
To smooth sand triumphant -
    until pounding foamy onslaught
        Wreaks chaos;
marauding granite, merciless wave crushes pleading shingle
        Fighting for its say;
Screaming seagulls crave attention
majestically gruesome - they scavenge for life
While gloomy crab desperately content with strife
        Sits, Apathetic.

And I, from my vantage point perceive the scene,
wondering at each blinded by its small world
Marvelling over the splendour,
    The Whole;
The meticulous rhythmic intricacy - master-minded;
And hope that I, in my small world
can look up to the greater - the Eternal -
to see the Beauty of the dimension we all share
which we must value and use
    To Love, to care;
the Truth is shown us, to fight towards - if we would;
Selfish striving turned through our insignificance
    To the One Great Goal of Good.

Clarence Shirky (18)
Bexhill College, Bexhill-on-Sea

Soul Cry

We stand in groups and stare alone,
Deep down inside, we face the unknown.
Forgive us, for we are running late,
To come knocking down Heaven's gate.

They forget both you and your sins,
While your fate never wins.
Show no mercy, show no love,
While our fate falls from high above.

Your knowledge and wisdom intertwined with rain,
To create the living soul of all pain.
The mysteries of life and the complexity,
What on earth does it have to do with me?

I cannot, I shan't ever let go,
When freedom shouts out to the count of zero.
Our lives - and deaths - begin to uncoil,
While we are still in a state of turmoil.

Our meanings and souls begin to cry
While we rot, and fade, and slowly die.

Alex Hunt (17)
Bexhill College, Bexhill-on-Sea

Ice Cream

I ce cream for hot days,
C ones in all different shapes and sizes.
E njoy all the flavours.

C old and delicious for summer days.
R aspberry ripple and chocolate chip.
E veryone can enjoy.
A mazing wafers you can have with your ice cream.
M elts in your mouth all day long.

Paige Lewis & Beth Goodwin (12)
Bishop Bell CE School, Eastbourne

Nasty

There once was a man with a bunion,
And he had himself an onion,
He thought it was sick,
So he ate it all quick,
And the juice made both his eyes run.

Jamie Fernandes
Bishop Bell CE School, Eastbourne

Ronaldo

R onaldo is the best player
O n the pitch he is the skill master
N o one can reach him, he's never in plaster
A gainst Liverpool, guess who will score
L ucky Ronaldo makes the ball soar
D amn! Five-nil
O h it's the end, five-nil, it finishes.

Grant Young (12)
Bishop Bell CE School, Eastbourne

The Food War

T he lettuce is torn to shreds.
H otter and hotter the oven gets.
E gg and bacon fries.

F ight to the finish,
O n the cooker,
O n the microwave.
D iced and sliced cut into small pieces.

W ater boiling.
A ll food juices squirting everywhere.
R acing, running for their lives.

Jake Yardley (13)
Bishop Bell CE School, Eastbourne

Chocolate Fondue

As I put the chocolate in
As I stir it round in the tin
As I watch it all go gloopy
It makes my mouth go wet and sloopy!

As I stab a little cherry
As I catch another berry
As I dip it in the pot
The chocolate burns me! Hot! Hot! Hot!

As it trickles down my chin
As it melts down within
As I glow, it's warm and scrummy
I love it so, it's *sooo* yummy!

Sally Bull (12)
Bishop Bell CE School, Eastbourne

Food Is Nice

F orever, food is very nice
O h yes, food is good
O verwhelming
D elicious

I rresistible
S crummy

N ever better
I ncredibly delicious
C hocolate is lovely
E veryone to enjoy.

Natasha Mizen (12)
Bishop Bell CE School, Eastbourne

Doughnut

The sugar from the doughnut melts on my hands.
Doughnuts come from many lands.
Doughnuts are fab for any girl or boy.
They come in lots of shapes for all to enjoy.
You enjoy it in the rain or shine
Even if you only have a little time!

Doris Loncarevic
Bishop Bell CE School, Eastbourne

Brian May

B rilliant
R ed guitar
I n Queen
A mazing guitarist
N ot straight hair that is everywhere

M agical when playing guitar
A lways good in tours
Y ippee! Uses a sixpence to play guitar.

Paul Morgan (12)
Bishop Bell CE School, Eastbourne

Food Family

My sister is like apple juice
I am allergic to it.

My mum is like hot curry
It's fiery when you try to chew it.

My dad is like lemons
They taste sour with a sweet aftertaste.

My nan is like sherry
It's dry but sometimes sweet.

My brother is like BBQ sauce
Its taste won't go away!

James Brindley (12)
Bishop Bell CE School, Eastbourne

Rory Bobson

R oyal Navy
O h so gory
R ed blood and guts
Y ellow sun, not so fun

B attleships ready
O cean waves crashing
B attleships *fire!*
S tunning jets flying
O ver the sea
N ot like anything you have ever seen!

Philip Hanaghan (12)
Bishop Bell CE School, Eastbourne

Chocolate

C hocolate fountains are the best
H ide it in your pocket or even your vest
O h my God, it's so divine
C hocolate, it's mine, mine, mine
O ops, it's all gone, I'm really bad
L ack of chocolate makes me mad
A ppetising sweetness, eat it for dessert
T reat your lover, it makes them flirt
E veryone loves it!

Tom Browning
Bishop Bell CE School, Eastbourne

Doughnuts

D elicious doughnuts. Chocolate ones are the best
O f course they're better than all the rest.
U sed are many different shapes
G et them cos they're better than tops
H ere they are, give them a try.
N utty, crunchy, they're better than pie.
U ndo the cover and eat them all up
T eeth bite into them and say *mmmm!*
S o here they are, don't waste time,
    Or I'll eat them all -
    And then they'll be mine!

Sophie Wren (12)
Bishop Bell CE School, Eastbourne

Queeny

Q uiet Queen, always smart,
U nique drawings of her, oh what good art,
E ats really slowly and has good health,
E veryone knows she has great wealth,
N o one knows what she does some days,
Y es, she's amazing, full of praise!

Tom Wilding
Bishop Bell CE School, Eastbourne

Ice Cream

I ce cream is nice for a girl or boy
C omes in different colours
E at it all day

C annot stop making a mess
R aspberry ripple delight
E at in the morning, all the way till night
A pple, pistachio, chocolate and vanilla
M ore ice cream is added to satisfy me.

Daniella Dolan
Bishop Bell CE School, Eastbourne

Fudge Cake

F ully loaded with chocolate
U nderstandably
D elicious, tastes
G orgeous when
E aten

C ake is eaten now
A gitated, it's all gone
K ipling (Mr)
E xceedingly good cakes.

Ben Farley
Bishop Bell CE School, Eastbourne

My Poem

Really hungry, I'm gonna starve
Dying for some food I had to sell my scarf
Now I'm living on fruit and veg
Then I stole a loaf of bread
I know it's bad, I don't usually steal
But I am getting far too ill
It was a case of life or death
Until I met a woman named Beth
She saved my life, I was close to my grave
Remember this woman she did, my life, save!

Lily Agg (12)
Bishop Bell CE School, Eastbourne

Ice Cream

I ce cream is tasty for everyone
C rispy chunks in some
E veryone's got to have one

C old and smooth, down your throat
R aisin and coffee, chocolate heaven
E at some at nine and more at eleven
A pple chunks and strawberry juice
M int fudge and vanilla mousse.

Adrianne Baumber (13)
Bishop Bell CE School, Eastbourne

Chocolate Cake!

I'm in my room at half nine
Thinking of you, how you're divine
I have an idea, I have a thought
But what happens if I'm caught?
I'll take a risk, I'll take a chance
Just thinking of you makes me dance
I creep outside my room at ten
My dad's asleep and so is Ben
I sneak downstairs, three at a time
Wondering if my plan is a crime
I cross the hall as it creaks
The hunter's here for what he seeks
I see a shadow, my heart misses a beat
Who is it? Who shall I meet?
My plan is ruined, for goodness sake!
It's Mum, tucking into to *my* cake!

Will Chrusciel (12)
Bishop Bell CE School, Eastbourne

A Lady Called Mary

There once was a lady called Mary
Who believed that she was a fairy
She used to make some spells
Out of water from Wells
She carried a wand in her bag
That she used as a flag
Now she is a fairy
'Cos she is so hairy.

Vicky Minty
Bishop Bell CE School, Eastbourne

Melons

M elons are delicious
E very bit suspicious
L ovely and fruity
O n a plate so fruity
N othing is so tasty
S o not as piece of pastry!

Isabelle Emery
Bishop Bell CE School, Eastbourne

Sweets

Sweets are lovely, sweets are sweet.
Gobstoppers, bubblegum, chocolates.
Every time I eat them I feel tingly
From my head to my feet.
Every day I eat sweets
Put it in my mouth
And give me a satisfying treat!

Mae Michaelson
Bishop Bell CE School, Eastbourne

Cheese

C heese is ever so tasty.
H ard is better than soft.
E at, eat, eat all day long.
E ating in the loft.
S coffing down the Cheddar.
E dam and Red Leicester.

I n comes Gloucester,
S melling ever so good.

G rating it up and putting on to the bread.
O n the cheese goes the ham.
O pen the fridge and get a drink.
D elicious was my lunch.

Daniel Harlow (13)
Bishop Bell CE School, Eastbourne

My Poem

C rispy and crunchy
R ough and tough
I n the cooker
S alt and vinegar
P lain and salted
Y ummy all the time

Charlie Steele
Bishop Bell CE School, Eastbourne

Untitled

My sister is like a tiger, pretty, strong and sharp-eyed
My kitten is a needle, she bites me every day
My dad is a dragon, he is so moody sometimes
And I am a cute bunny, but when you get me angry be ready
                                                    for a scare.

Bryony Wilkinson
Bishop Bell CE School, Eastbourne

Meat

Led up to the steel doors
I look upon the dusty floor
With all the meat laid here before me
Flowing through my mind.

The field I know is long behind
And tears will fill my family's eyes
A struggle would be hopeless now
I see it is my time.

And now, inside the fearful dark
The cold machinery will start
Create another sack of meat
For the stomachs of Mankind.

Lee Glenister
Bishop Bell CE School, Eastbourne

Acrostic

S ugary, satisfying
W hat type are you buying?
E verybody needs a treat
E ven if you cheat
T empting sweets
S o you can just eat and eat!

Amanda Buckwell & Larissa Burgess (13)
Bishop Bell CE School, Eastbourne

Through The Eyes Of Randomness

Windows look, bananas peel,
shoes squeak, mice squeal.

Snotty hankies, clean socks,
people bawling, boxers box.

Dry land, wet feet,
combed hair, drumming beat.

White teeth, clocks tick,
This poem's getting on my wick!

Tabitha Hilton-Berry & Amy Lambert (13)
Claverham Community College, Battle

Through The Eyes Of A Mirror

My life is dark and lonely
The days pass as I sit on the wall
Every day is a nervous wait
I know I'm going to fall.

My glittering image beckons them all,
They come at a racing pace,
Flicks of lipgloss and foundation
Smeared on my face.

Some days I'm useful some days I'm not,
But the people are always vain,
Skinny, ugly, pretty or fat,
You can count on them to complain.

At the end of the day I hang in silence,
Listening to the hush,
A rectangular box in darkness
Awaiting the morning rush.

Ellie Casey (13)
Claverham Community College, Battle

Through The Eyes Of . . .

Every day it sees the same things.
Running and hopping around in circles.
The same garden,
The same scene.

It feels trapped

The walls of the run stand tall,
Keeping it inside the same enclosed space.
It wants to break free,
It wants to see the world.

It starts to dig,
It digs and burrows for days.
Under the fence it's crawling,
And at last it's escaped.

She's free.
She can see everything so clearly now,
Instead of staring through wires.
The world is so big to her,
She can explore and wonder . . .

Alicia Russell (14)
Claverham Community College, Battle

Through The Eyes Of A Snail

I crawl stickily over the grass,
Though it's more in the grass,
Than on the grass,
I'm so small.
I wave my muscular neck,
Looking around at my surroundings.
Grass.

Oh how boring, how monotonous.
It's pretty dull, very dull.
Resigned to the fact
That I'm only ever going to be a snail,
I sigh, and move on
To more grass.
I gradually make my way
To a point in the near distance.
But it's only more grass.

So I try to cheer myself up.
I wiggle my antennae,
This could be fun!
But I assure you it's *not.*
I try crawling up a tree,
But I fall back down
Into the grass.
Ugh, what a boring and unfulfilling life I lead.
I slowly crawl, thoroughly depressed, on.
I look up
And see a slug.
It could be worse!

India Jones (13)
Claverham Community College, Battle

Hide White Space

I'm always there,
Like a distant and unwanted shadow,
And you're always told,
To hide the white space because
A book with white pages says nothing,
And a poster that is blank earns no money.

I'm there but you don't see me,
As a sky defines its horizon,
I'm part of the world around you,
In your face; so close
That I'm filtered out,
Fading from the foreground.

I'm blank,
So I'm unoriginal, you may think,
Not special or hot.
But like air to your breath, I'm the oxygen.
Take me away and you'll have everything,
Yet nothing left.

Rachel Meehan (13)
Claverham Community College, Battle

The Seasons

The frost is settling after its long journey,
The harsh wind freezes our faces,
The snowman across the road smiles broadly at me.
We shiver and shake and huddle together
As winter takes it toll.

The lambs are skipping with glee across the lush grass,
The tulips are stretching high, displaying their ruby-red crowns.
The trees are awakening after their long winter sleep,
The smiling sun gently warms the world below.
And the chirpy children run and play,
As the land begins to smile.

The roasting red sun blazes and roars,
The families flock to the soft, shady beaches,
The aroma of barbecues sweeps across the garden,
The freshly mown grass shimmers and shines.
The panting dog sleeps in the shade,
As his fur coat hugs round him tightly.

The browns and reds stick to the landscape,
The flustered trees shake off their garments.
The busy squirrels prepare for the winter.
The wispy wind makes a tornado of leaves,
The grizzly children rub and pat their heads,
As the crisp conkers fall from above.

Jodie Powell (13)
Claverham Community College, Battle

Through The Eyes Of . . .

Here I sit,
Alone,
Observing,
Watching life pass,
Listening to the birds' whistle,
Sunrays beating on my leaves,
Sky darkening,
The clouds give way,
And burst into a million tiny droplets of rain,
Grumbling thunder is heard,
Refreshing for me,
Animals scuttle desperately across the lush, green grassland.
Once over, all is silent,
Drip, drip, drip,
The birds fill the sky once again,
I feel fresh and ready for the long years to come,
Sitting here,
Being me,
Yeah . . . that's right, *just that tree.*

William Cousins (13)
Claverham Community College, Battle

Through The Eyes Of A Cat

Clouds swirl slowly in the sky,
I allow them to unfold and float away.
They are in my power and at my command,
They entertain me, as in the grass I lay.

I hunt and terrorise spiders and moths,
To protect the family in my house.
They need me and feed me and groom my fur,
Grateful for the gift of a half-eaten mouse.

The birds swoop bravely over me,
As I stretch my limbs out long.
Taunting me with their twittering chatter,
I could easily end their days, but my fatigue is too strong.

Freya Josling (13)
Claverham Community College, Battle

The Meaning Of Life

T eaching and learning.
H alf full or half empty?
E xciting.

M ake tea not war.
E ndangered.
A lpha to omega.
N oumonoultramicroscopicsilvolcanicconunosis.
I nteresting.
N ew beginnings, old end.
G od, the almighty!

O pen debate.
F ood, *ummmmm* doughnuts.

L ove.
I ntellectual.
F amily and friends.
E gg or chicken? You decide!

Ethan Greenwood (14)
Claverham Community College, Battle

Through The Eyes Of The Third World

They gaze at people,
Walking across the litter-laden street,
Glaring hungrily at the hamburgers and
Chips that we carry.

With our back pockets full of change,
We scurry past, showered with hopeful
And innocent glances.

Misted with tears as they evoke their
Childhood, riddled with choices and
Paths.
They took the wrong one . . .

Leftover food is left to be fought over,
Against the birds while the lucky ones
Busk and beg.

They don't want much
God Bless.

Dan Finley (14)
Claverham Community College, Battle

Through The Eyes Of . . . Duvet Dave

Stuck in the overflowing estuaries of the city.
Stuck in the dribs and drabs of life.
The coppers of the common man.

My hat, my work,
My guitar, my implement,
My pavement, my duvet,
No money,
No smokes.

The repetitive tune.
The repetitive tune of life.
The repetitive ruptures of squalor.
Duvet Dave.

Laurence Flint (13)
Claverham Community College, Battle

Through The Eyes Of . . . A Monkey In A Zoo

The sinister faces press up against my glass enclosure
It looks like I can touch them
Like I can get out; be free
But every time I reach, the cold, hard reality stops me

Sometimes I sit and watch
With no energy, the will to fulfil life drained
I watch the people, big, small, all staring
Sizing me and my family up; comparing.

Why they care I do not know
Most of the time we just think about what our lives could be
If those heartless humans didn't capture
Could our lives be happiness and rapture?

The different people we watch
Most look happy to see us
Some look sad to see us ensnared in glass
Would you if you saw my aunt rocking back and forth,
                                    ripping out grass?

My daddy tells me I will find a way out some day
And start my own family in the wild
But I know the malevolent hunters will trap us again
So we're stuck, never to feel sunlight, never to feel rain

Are we just a circus act?
Here for only entertainment?
To stay while glass closes in?
While we watch faces sneer, while ours are like devils sick of sin?

Georgina Hale (14)
Claverham Community College, Battle

Through The Eyes Of . . .

You are my crutch, my friend
You seem to hold all the answers
Help me go on
You build me up
Knock me down
Numb the pain
Help me escape
Make it better
But once the ecstasy is gone
I'm back again
Square one
I try to control you but, of course, you control me
I tell myself I can do without you
But you draw me back in
You're the most beautiful thing in the world
The only thing I need
But you make it all worse
Why can't I quit you?
I'll quit you -
But just one last time . . .

Louisa Maycock (13)
Claverham Community College, Battle

Through The Eyes Of . . . A Broken Heart

In agony for love,
Painful memories replay every day,
As I beat and beat,
Faster and faster,
Knowing this suffering is endless.
When will this torture end?

I struggle for what feels an eternity,
I can't stop,
I'm helpless, hopeless,
I beat, I pump,
Over and over, but I cannot mend!

Like an open wound which will not heal,
I can't be helped,
Only time will tell,
But time just hurts more and more,
Second by second,
Day by day,
Month by month . . .

Abbie Hyman (14)
Claverham Community College, Battle

Through The Eyes Of This Bottle

Through the eyes of this bottle,
Is something unknown.
Such a deep life,
Being a slave to the confused captivator,
That holds you so close.
You must be so sick of the shallowness,
Of the emptiness of their soul.
Yet it is their life,
They can take you as they wish.
They may think you are the cure,
You are the only thing that keeps them high.
But then you can watch them fall,
Lower than they were before.
You can seem the most beautiful,
Enchanting thing in the world.
But then you capture them,
They can never seem to let you go.
You are the medicine for someone that is already cured.
You are the introduction to someone's darkness.
You are the heart to someone's soul.
But more often than not you burn them,
You brand them so everyone can see.
They come to you for the answers,
That you have never known.

Hannah Caney (13)
Claverham Community College, Battle

Through The Eyes Of . . .

Dead trees line the fraying paths,
The quiet birdsong no longer issues,
Nothing moves.
Darkness frames the horizon.
All wind has gone,
The trees no longer sway.
Clouds hang draped over the mountaintops.
White fading to grey,
Grey fading to black.
And I am gone.

Xenia Millar (13)
Claverham Community College, Battle

Through The Eyes Of Light

I am the one,
That makes people feel safe,
I am the one,
That strengthens people's faith,
I am the one,
That warms creatures' hearts,
I am the one,
That defeats the dark,
I am the one,
That has been here for centuries past,
I am the one,
That travels really fast,
I am the one,
That brings hope to men,
I am the one,
That warms up your den,
I am the one,
That brightens up the room,
I am the one,
That will be here again, soon,
I am the one,
That extends your sight,
I am the one,
I am the light.

Thomas Maryan (13)
Claverham Community College, Battle

Through The Eyes Of A Fast Food Table

I sit here
awaiting the rush.
The new and the old,
the shy and the bold.
Like cows they come here to graze,
as they buy their deaths,
They sit down and put it on me.
I feel the grease and fat dripping on me,
I hold my breath as they open theirs up,
and pull chunks off.
No manners.
No honour.
They sit *chomping,*
Chomping,
Chomping.
I see the children grabbing their lunches
and I wish that they'd go away,
away from the death.
Make something of their lives.
But they carry on
destroying their bodies.
As they *chomp,*
Chomp,
Chomp.

Alex Merrick (13)
Claverham Community College, Battle

Home Sweet Home

A snail can't say, home sweet home,
Because it's on his back.
He will always be very safe,
Flying his Union Jack.

He says it's hard to hoover,
With his house on his back,
He says the cleaning's easy,
Once you've got the knack!

It's useful for TV he says,
I'm always up to date,
Because I'm always at my house,
I'm never, never late!

He says there are advantages,
Of carrying your home,
Except of course for the loneliness,
Of living all alone!

And finally, to end his song,
It's really not a joke,
Please stop those children picking me up,
And giving me a poke!

Zoë Kirkwood (13)
Claverham Community College, Battle

Through The Eyes Of The Sea

Waiting as the world goes by,
Slowly and endlessly going on,
Since the dawn of time I've been here,
Going from country to country, meeting all.
I drift shore to shore, in and out,
As I am moved by the tide.

I endure the world using me as a tool,
From transport to fun,
I want to be one of them,
Just one day to be human, to know what it's like,
Why do humans treat me this way?
Could someone else take my place?

Sometimes I get angry,
Why should I be tortured?
It's somebody else's turn now,
I will pluck every boat upon me,
Let them know my wrath and give them a place
In my murky depths.

I am calm after I'm angry,
The world seems to let out a sigh of relief,
And makes my heart feel lighter,
I like to gleam with the help of the sun,
I can't be angry, I'm just too nice,
But my brothers, that's another matter.

I am the sea, proud and strong,
Let that be known to all,
I deserve some goodness in my life,
While I serve, for our Mother Earth.

Lewis Saunders (13)
Claverham Community College, Battle

Through The Eyes Of A Dustbin Lid

That's all I'm good for,
Bang.
I'm just a cover.
Not a real thing in its own right.

They say I talk rubbish,
But if I didn't who would?
They don't think I deserve freedom,
But they are wrong.

I would like a house in Spain as much as the next lid,
But to do I get one?
No.
I would like free health care on the NHS.
But did I get it?
No.
And I would like to go about without getting
Funny looks.
But do I get that?
No.

Bang!

Lydia Bell (13)
Claverham Community College, Battle

The Eyes Of An Eyewitness

I saw it.
No blood in the ballroom,
Or with the spanner in the kitchen
The dead night is filled with gloom
As blue lights flash
And sirens whine.
Behind us, hours back, guests arrive,
They wine and dine.
Not knowing.

I saw him.
Blended in with the background behind him
He acts as a shadow
His presence dull and dim.
Excusing himself, he leaves the table
I follow him outside
His cloak, the colour of sable
Sweeps the floor.
He has a job to do.

I saw where . . .
The glint of metal shines like a warning signal, danger was coming.
I know I have to stop him. See his face
Before it is too late.
But he runs inside, the lights go out
I knew it would happen, I run.
A slash, a slump, a shout,
He got away,
But I saw his face.

Philippa Wiggins (13)
Claverham Community College, Battle

Blind

Every day I hear the sound of evil, no pictures to make me understand.
Maybe you can't understand something which is so strong
in this world.

I hear men fighting in streets without names, always someone
close by me,
hiding the truth of the dark, smelly alley.
The one which I walk down, not knowing what's going on around me.

Maybe men are just joking, but how would I know what joking is?
I see no feelings. I just hear them.
Always bad feelings but no good pictures.
I have no friends that I can see.
Just hear their voices but anger fills their voices up with hatred
for this world.

No one understands what I'm feeling, they just make me bottle
it up inside.
They do not talk about bad, they lie to me, say it's all OK.
I cannot see but I can sense.
I want to shout but who would care anyway?
I'm nothing, no one, just one more person in this world.
They don't need me, they don't want me.

I could go and they wouldn't notice.
But how can I go,
I am blind.

Mae Harris (11)
Dorothy Stringer School, Brighton

Where Did All The Flowers Go?

Where did all the flowers go?
When did they disappear?
Who killed them?
When?
And why?
When was the last time you gazed at the intricate detail
In the flower of a rose?
Was the rose in a field or a book?
Where did all the flowers go?
Who waters them now?
Why not?
Flowers are not things to fuss over,
They are things to admire, respect, cherish.
Every time someone picked a wild flower
It was just another dagger pushed into the heart of the Earth.
Where did all the flowers go?
If only I knew . . .

Bethany Coomber (12)
Dorothy Stringer School, Brighton

Black

Jus' 'cos I black don't mean I'm bad
I'm tall up for ma age
I'm a skinhead
I wear my brudders cloths
But jus' 'cos I black don't mean I'm bad
I aint got a good eddication
Mi pa aint around
Mi ma's a rat
But jus' 'cos I black don't mean I'm bad
Beasts don't think so
I can't be anywhere without them eyein' me down
Checkin' mi pockets
But jus' 'cos I black don't mean I'm bad
White mudders cross da street to 'void me
Shielding they're youfs
Like am a duippie wit da pleg
But all da time I know it int cos I'm bad.

Rosie Bergonzi (13)
Dorothy Stringer School, Brighton

Anger

The fire lit the cave all around
The purple ivy clung to the walls
A stag strutted majestically around.
And lo! Over by the doorway, Anger.
In red cloak and trident stands.
She stands tall. Stands brave.
Her eyes gleaming, observant, her smile a sneer.
In full ruby glare.
Besides her sit two men in chains of fire.
Their eyes covered with a monobrow of fieriness.
Their red clothes torn off the shoulder.
Their eyes bruised and bloodshot.
The voices gone, with the noises.
The crackle of the fire was the only laughter.

Kirsty Bird (13)
Dorothy Stringer School, Brighton

But My Love Is Stronger

Eyes like sapphires on a ring on a hand waved in the moonlight
But my love for him is more beautiful
Hair like the rarest, softest russet-coloured silk
But my love for him is gentler
Skin like the sweetest milkiest chocolate
But my love for him is more delicious
Lips like the softest winter-ripe berries
But my love is sweeter

Dancing, graceful and enticing
But my love for him is more poised
Laughter, a chorus of soprano bells
But my love for him is more musical

He may be beautiful and sweet
But if he wasn't, my love for him wouldn't change
Because we are in love
And love is stronger.

Robyn Jury (13)
Dorothy Stringer School, Brighton

My Generation

My generation is a prison,
With a sentence that will last forever,
The lives of humans make little difference,
As any one of their endeavours.

My life is insignificant,
Or that's what I've been taught,
And the beliefs of every martyr,
Should be constrained and fought.

A silent poet's weeping,
Over his own forgotten grave,
Dug by a generation,
That's made his soul a slave.

A worker slaves for all his life,
But how will this be shown?
By an almost deserted funeral,
And a second-hand tombstone.

Jacob Harris (13)
Dorothy Stringer School, Brighton

The Hidden Power

The owner of this world is hidden,
Something of which we will never be ridden,
Yet it is all around us,
Timing us as we catch the bus.

It's in London, Greenwich and New York,
Timing you as you pull out a cork,
Everyone is governed by it,
It is even there when you sit.

This hidden power has been called time,
Timing me as I write this rhyme,
Something on which Americans wouldn't spend a dime,
Drinking coconut added to lime.

All too soon your time is up,
Like drinking poison from a cup,
Time ticks away your life,
Cutting through you like a knife.

Fraser Greenroyd (15)
Frewen College, Nr Hastings

The Outdoor Autumn

I am savouring my sweet toffee apple,
Birds are twittering in the skies,
As rain drops from the tree,
People carving ripe pumpkins for Hallowe'en,
Farmer picking golden crops.

Wind blowing the leaves away . . .
Clouds cover the sunlight,
Vines twisting on fences,
Cold and warm all at once.

Soft wind on my face,
Wet ground being trodden on,
Heaps of horse chestnuts,
Greedy children's horde collected conkers,
Squelchy footsteps fading and fading . . .

Pantira Mahattanyavanit (11)
Our Lady of Sion School, Worthing

Autumn Life

Autumn walks slowly through the tall red trees.
Every step spreads a wave of mists and new ripe fruit
Across the orchard.

Bright orange leaves crunching under my feet,
Big red apples and piano music
In the distance.

Small dark acorns and squirrels searching for sweet chestnuts,
Dark green leaves and I know that
Christmas is coming.

George Richey (11)
Our Lady of Sion School, Worthing

Autumn

Orange, red and amber glow,
Burnished by the sun so low.

Rustling leaves, swaying trees,
Dancing dreamily in the breeze.

The garden's carpet re-laid,
A pattern of golden acorns.

As summer fades away,
Autumn comes to stay.

Until winter will enter on icy wings,
And stamp out the joys of autumn.

Lucy Baker (11)
Our Lady of Sion School, Worthing

Autumn Poem

Leaves falling from trees,
Scattering with the wind,
Apples drop swiftly to the ground,
Light winds flow through fingers,
Soft winds tap at trees,
Magic in the air,
Small birds, winter's refugees,
Squirrels chomp chestnuts,
Lively scent of flowers,
Fragrant apple pies,
Late fruits, still juicy,
Feel them squash in your fingers,
Birds still singing love songs,
Flapping in a puddle bath,
Drops of rain cascade from branches,
Leaves flinch in the wind,
Swaying trees dance to the wind's music,
Small puddles ripple in silence.

Danielle Jones (11)
Our Lady of Sion School, Worthing

Autumn

Morning dew glistens,
Trees sway and dry leaves rustle,
Spiky conker shells roll along the ground
Like stinging nettles,
Blowing in the wind,
Rain trickles down the windowpane.

Toffee apples gleam like sunlight,
Birds trill and branches sway,
Carpet of leaves dampening,
Puddles deep and murky.

Autumn trees dancing freely like droopy willows
In the crisp, refreshing breeze,
Mists linger,
Mossed branches dampen and clouds close in
As darkness appears.

Jessica Stubbs (11)
Our Lady of Sion School, Worthing

Autumn Snapshots

Rolling fields gilded
By a glowing sun.
Cloudless sky, horizon to horizon.
A boy sits on his tree swing,
Leaf and apple carpets
Fill the land.
Crumbles with custard fill stomachs.
Strings of conkers clash,
Hide-and-seek amid eerie woods
And chase by sparkling stream.
Webs glinting with dew
Are bridges between bushes.

James Cowley (11)
Our Lady of Sion School, Worthing

Autumn Thoughts

Brown, crispy leaves tumbling from trees,
wispy clouds in the sky,
wind swirling through trees,
red apples resting amongst the leaves.

Trees undressing, losing all colour,
puddles waiting,
the last birds of autumn chatting,
as robins take their place.

Hope Maddocks (11)
Our Lady of Sion School, Worthing

Autumn Thoughts

A time of peace and rich colours,
A time of happiness, fiery flowers,
A time of crisp, nut-brown oak trees,
Apple trees bending low with ripe fruit.

Sweet aromas of plump red apples,
The air filled with sweet smells,
As the smell of fat, juicy pumpkins hits your nose,
On a cold, damp, dying day.

Feeling of joy and laughter,
And cold freshness,
Feeling of dew under your feet,
A slight breeze, as damp leaves drift.

Soft chirruping of birds,
Rain splashing off trees,
Drip! Drip! Drip!
As long branches hang low.

Sarah Gregory (11)
Our Lady of Sion School, Worthing

Signs Of Autumn

The rustle of leaves,
Birds singing in some trees,
Water gliding down long winding streams,
A plane soars across the sky.

The vivid, golden sun,
Spiders on shiny, spiralling webs,
And Guy Fawkes ablaze on a stick!

Juicy, ripe blackberries.
Smooth, glossy toffee apples.

A soft breeze on my cheeks,
Leaves crunch under my feet.

Autumn exists and winter enters!

Beau Hayes (11)
Our Lady of Sion School, Worthing

Autumn - Season Of Colour

Chestnuts with spiky shells;
Leisurely rolling away.
Leaves, gold, crimson and auburn;
Rest and curl, drooping on their vast hazel seats.
Blackberries, black and blue;
Like bruises in verdant bushes.
Bay leaves, fragrant,
Crushed to let out a sweet, minty fragrance . . .

Owl twittering at night;
Waking you suddenly.
Baked apples oozing mince;
Cloaked in custard.
Kids in costumes;
Collecting sweets!
Pumpkins, evil and orange;
Glowing red and yellow . . .

Spiders on shiny webs;
Imprison their prey.
Autumn sun against my face;
Turning into a blasting wind.
Puddles, dark, dingy, muddy;
Underneath, like a chest, no one knows what's inside . . .

Chestnuts dangling from trees;
Like bonbons on a Christmas tree.

Elliot Gamble (11)
Our Lady of Sion School, Worthing

A Touch Of Autumn

Birds gliding gracefully overhead,
Droplets falling on my head,
The musky autumn smell,
Leaves rustling in the breeze,
Dried by the constant wind.

Grass swaying gently in the breeze,
Leaves turning to crisp curls,
Wind moaning,
Days shortening,
Animals in deep sleep.

A duvet of leaves on autumn's floor,
Trees throwing out their old clothes,
Puddles dimpled by the wind's breath,
Calming clouds,
Once blue seas are now white waves.

Jack Ravan (12)
Our Lady of Sion School, Worthing

Autumn Poem

Red leaves fluttering through the air,
Prickly chestnuts descend from the trees,
Daring boys rolling in the mud,
Some birds flee.

Others defy the cold weather,
Squirrels collect their nuts,
Feathers fall on hedgehog,
Settling down to hibernate.

Long green grass covered by red leaves,
Snails trail on the wall,
Sun glistens on a wet spiderweb,
Birds pick red berries.

Robert Ford (11)
Our Lady of Sion School, Worthing

Autumn Forever

Apple trees burdened with heavy branches,
Big, golden apples waiting to plummet down to Earth;
Fields bursting with life,
The clear blue sky sparkles down on Earth,
Ripe autumn is here.

Crunching leaves, echoes in the air,
Birds chattering, interrupting each other,
Twisting spiralling trees.

Clouds are drifting by,
The sun grows old.

Tom Crocker (11)
Our Lady of Sion School, Worthing

Autumn

Trees wafting in the whirling wind,
Dancing to autumn's songs,
Fat, glossy blackberries,
Rosy red apple trees warped with bulky ripeness
Ground smothered in reds, browns, yellows.
Tiny acorns waiting to become massive trees,
Dogs bolting through fields of tall grass,
Birds gossiping in trees,
About things we don't understand.
The sweet aroma of a pie in the oven,
Glossy puddles reflect a clear blue sky,
Red berries shining in the maturing sun.
Spiderwebs sparkling with raindrops.

Elsie Steinmore (11)
Our Lady of Sion School, Worthing

An Autumn Afternoon

A gentle wind,
But . . . fresh, warming.
Gorgeous apples,
Plump and fiery red.

Gazing upon the beauty of autumn.
Leaves rustling everywhere.
Smell of crisp autumn air.

Cobwebs brushing on my legs,
Smell of a bonfire.
Leaves swirling on the ground.

Suddenly they stop.
It's night-time,
There is a change in the air.
Branches swaying vigorously.
The ear-piercing whistle of the wind.

It all stops, and I know,
Autumn and I have to wait,
To enjoy each other's company again.

Emma Sexton (12)
Our Lady of Sion School, Worthing

Autumn

Out comes the sun
And a soft breeze
Blowing all the apples off the trees
Big, juicy red ones falling on the damp floor
Leaves rustle whilst animals fumble across golden fields
Day is no more as the sun goes down
Fresh smells, warm nights
Birds' soft tweets echo around
Then quiet
Lights off
Doors closed
Spider webs glistening in the moonlight
Trees standing bare as their leaves are shed
All around is dull now that winter is here.

Ryan Wootton (12)
Our Lady of Sion School, Worthing

Autumn

Autumn has begun with bundles of joy,
Golden leaves drop from the trees.
Spiders spin their glorious webs,
Children clamber up the trees.

The cold breeze blows on my face,
Fruits of autumn fresh and ripe,
Chestnuts tumble from the trees.
Harvest has come.

Leaves crunch beneath my feet;
The journey has ended,
Winter has begun,
Christmas, here we come!

James Cairns (11)
Our Lady of Sion School, Worthing

Autumn

The beaches lay empty and quiet,
Once busy water parks drained and closed.
Birds gather, excitedly, all of a twitter,
Ready to fly south, away from wind that is bitter.

Spiders and craneflies stir and venture out,
Spinning delicate webs and joyfully fluttering about.
Trees and crops mature and ripe,
Harvested before drawing night.

Conkers and chestnuts tumble from the trees,
Red, crunchy leaves dance happily around my knees.
Jack Frost is showing his chilliness,
By tingling and reddening my nose.

I do love the changes that autumn brings;
The colours, the coldness and everything.

James Hall (11)
Our Lady of Sion School, Worthing

Autumn

A watery sun seeps through clouds in shimmering strips,
Morning fogs and mists lie heavily in the air.
Hedgehogs crawl across the lawn,
Lazy dragonflies and bumblebees hover casually.

Squirrels search for acorns,
To set aside for hibernation,
Scurrying through the crunchy leaves,
Across the forest floor.

Animals await the late sun,
Tempted to rest again.
The mice poke out their heads
The robin is the next guest.

The strong old oak stretches its arms in silence,
With twists and turns from roots to branch ends,
A golden sea; no grass in sight,
Not to be green until spring arrives.

Evergreens tower over those who are losing their cloaks of colour,
Damp, pungent leaves decay on the path,
Northern winds blow down great leaves,
Amber leaves float and swirl, never in a straight line.

Jessica Gander (11)
Our Lady of Sion School, Worthing

Autumn

Season of mist and haze,
Birds chorus in the trees.
Children leap into leaves,
Their laughter fills the air.

A dazzling sun glows,
Trees tremble and quiver.
Spiders webs glisten,
Leaves tumble to the ground.

Prickly shells of conkers;
Ready to prick innocent victims,
Cold wind stings my face.
Scent of bay leaves floats around.

Emma White (12)
Our Lady of Sion School, Worthing

Autumn Poem

Cold breeze brushing past my cheeks,
Moist air making me feel wet;
Grass squelching beneath my feet,
And spots of rain speckling my neck.

Cold, fresh air on my tongue,
Chestnuts heating on a fire;
Sweetness from home-made toffee apples,
Safety and warmth of a pot of tea.

The sweet fragrance of a bay leaf tree,
Pleasant smells of fully grown flowers;
Fresh, mellow, succulent fruit,
And ripeness from a fresh gourd.

Leaves rustle as they flutter down,
Hear bumps when apples tumble to the ground;
Birds sing and swoop above,
And trees sway in gentle winds.

Fresh colours of an autumn garden,
Bare trees from which the leaves have fallen;
Vines wrap around fences and walls,
And hedges grow wildly around.

Rachel Watson (10)
Our Lady of Sion School, Worthing

Autumn

Spiky conker shells
Bunched up like tiny green hedgehogs.
Golden apples
Dangle from branches.
Over-ripe pears drown in the grass;
Early Christmas decorations.
Magpies and swallows
Waiting for the last word;
To depart from the departure lounge full of . . .
Squeals and cheeps.
Crisp mornings and shorter evenings.
A slight breeze whispering to the leaves,
Crispy and red,
Littering the forest floor.
Autumn packing its suitcase!

Eleanor Church (11)
Our Lady of Sion School, Worthing

Autumn To Winter

I sense that autumn's here by now,
With the crisp leaves off the bare branches.
I feel the bitterness of the cold slowly trickling down my spine.
The moist ground squelching under my feet.

My lips shrivelled up,
Waiting for a toffee apple to rescue them.
I hear the birds twitter in the sky,
In and out of the empty trees.

When the fireworks crackle and spit,
I'm warming up to a hot, scorching bonfire,
And Guy is relaxing on a red-hot fire.
Whilst crisp leaves are swooping down from the trees,
And sizzling up like bacon in a pan.
The bonfire has started to smoulder,
Like when a kettle has boiled.

Christmas is coming as fast as you could ever imagine.
It won't be long now.

Katie Goulder (12)
Our Lady of Sion School, Worthing

Autumn

Birds awakening from their nests,
Chirping in the blue sky,
Oak trees swaying in the breeze,
Conkers tumbling, green and prickly.
Grass wet and dewy.

I breathe the cold air,
Clouds form from my mouth.
The gentle morning breeze,
Strokes my face,
Leaves sweep the ground.

Fond memories of horses galloping,
Through bright, red poppies,
Covered in mist.

Warm stew, juicy dumplings,
Slouching in the lounge,
Strudel and cream.
Rain tapping at my window,
Warm, cosy fire,
Quiet and dozy.

Emma Blurton (11)
Our Lady of Sion School, Worthing

Autumn Time

Autumn is here, summer has gone
Leaves turn brown
Then tumble down to the chalky ground below.
It is the season for roast
With apple pie, I cherish the most
Conker season
Mysterious spiders dance on their webs.
Days become shorter
Newly formed puddles swirling with water
Boys climb trees
Fall down and hurt themselves.

Hallowe'en; apple bobbing and candle flare
Witches and ghosts haunt the night.
Cold November Bonfire Night
Spectacular fireworks fill crowds with wonder
Autumn ends
Another season passed in our lives.

Lawrence Thompson (11)
Our Lady of Sion School, Worthing

Autumn

Sitting on the school wall, the birds dive-bombing for food,
Scared spiders running quickly along their webs.

A gentle breeze tickles my face.
The branches, swaying, leaves fluttering quickly to the ground,
Forming brown swirling piles around my feet.

The birds jabbering, quarrelling like an old married couple,
Visiting neighbours.

Time to leave, just like summer!

Tom Dolby (11)
Our Lady of Sion School, Worthing

Autumn's Ways

As summer begins to cease
And it grows colder
Conkers fall off trees
And time gets older

Golden leaves engulf the floor
Squirrels carry nuts in their jaw
And fruit begins to grow
As if it will never say no

Nights become longer
Roots get stronger
The trees are bare
As autumn is standing there
With leaves all around him.

Dominic Clough-Whelan (12)
Our Lady of Sion School, Worthing

Amazing Autumn

Quiet mists of the season settle,
Getting colder by the day.
As the birds start chattering,
Flying high, for their long journey.

Trees bow, heavy with fruit,
And natural fragrances are in command.
Insects and small mammals settle in,
For the long, long night to come.

A drowsy sun,
Light starting to fade.
Frost dusts the land,
Winter again!

Gareth Ettridge (11)
Our Lady of Sion School, Worthing

How Autumn Works

Leaves rustling in the breeze,
Trees bare,
All quiet, no sound,
Until children come to play.
Chestnuts! Conkers!
Who's got the most?

Autumn like a colour chart,
Red, yellow, brown and green.
A light mist in the air.

Muffled in scarves, kicking through leaves,
Birds chattering in trees,
A robin redbreast singing softly.
A warm dinner,
The smooth sweetness of a . . .
Toffee apple.
A smouldering fire,
Drifting into sleep.

Emma Roberts (11)
Our Lady of Sion School, Worthing

School Is Always Hard

When I go to school
I always feel real cool.
But when I see the work
I shudder and I jerk.
The lessons are too hard
I'm always on my guard
(In case I get it wrong).
I always try my best
And I'm as good as all the rest.

Kelly Gunn (13)
Patcham House School, Brighton

School

You start your day with fear
It makes you shed a tear
At first it's great and new
Next just something to do
Your lessons are a drag
Your teacher is a hag
The rest of the day you moan
Till it's time for you to go home.

Samuel Humphrey (14)
Patcham House School, Brighton

Pizza

You buy your pizza hot
It has herbs that like dots
It is good to bite
Its cheese so thick and light
You leave it in the box
Whilst you turn to chase a fox
But it turns into mould
When it becomes too old.

Evan Hilton (13)
Patcham House School, Brighton

Cinquain - Stations

Stations
PlayStation games
Then come boxed in cardboard
When my mum shouted up the stairs
Come down!

Nathan Rushin (13)
Patcham House School, Brighton

Casualty

Chasing through the lights
To A and E at night
At first alert and keen
Later they're shattered and mean
They must reach the ice
(They have to save a life)
They learn to their despair
That life's not always fair.

David Hall (13)
Patcham House School, Brighton

Friends

You think you're all alone
Having a whine and a moan
But then someone nice and kind
Tells you it's going to be fine
Then to your feet you get
With someone you've just met
Then you learn in a year or ten
All you needed was a friend.

Leanne Dearling (13)
Patcham House School, Brighton

Christmas

Lots of gifts ready for
The tree
Santa
Comes sliding
Down the chimney
Rudolph is ready and
Waiting too
They set off to every
House in town
Visiting
Everywhere
They can
Dropping toys and gifts down
The chimney.

Daniel Ford (13)
Patcham House School, Brighton

This Is Just To Say

That I didn't
Mean to
Kick my ball
At the
Window

And I
Am sorry for
Throwing
My frisbee

Forgive me
Because I
Mean to
And I'm sorry.

Harry Dale (11)
Patcham House School, Brighton

Haikus

The white snow is thick
Like shimmering dust, keeping
The bare trees frozen

Pebbles on the beach
The ocean makes them sparkle
Semi-precious stones.

Unthinkable wave
Came suddenly and destroyed.
Horrifying pain!

Kaia Hancock (12)
Patcham House School, Brighton

Cinquain - Game Boy

Game Boy
Very noisy
Challenging, frustrating
Playing it quietly, alone
Time out.

Gregory Hedges (11)
Patcham House School, Brighton

Dragon - Cinquain

Dragon
Fire burning bright
Flying, gliding, landing
Courageously fighting battles
Fighter.

Joanne Lloyd (11)
Patcham House School, Brighton

The World's A Psychedelic Place

The world is a psychedelic place to be born
If you don't mind the world spinning at your feet
If drugs are the only solution to your problems
And the Earth has abolished all traces of meat
Are there anymore of these around . . .?
Obviously not.

The world is a psychedelic place to be born
If only you saw colours twirling in the air
With your clothes all dirty and unwashed hair
The world is a very peaceful place to be . . .
For some of us.

The world is a psychedelic place to be born
If people would be brave and wear beautiful flowers
Sing and dance for several hours
The world is a very heavy place
Well . . . for hippies.

Joseph Cooke (14)
Patcham House School, Brighton

The World Is A Beautiful Place

The world is a beautiful place
    If you desire to follow your dreams
If you don't mind not enjoying the one love
    If you love to watch your child grow

The world is a beautiful place
    If you love listening to the sound of life
If you don't mind a love affair watching the sky
    If you don't mind failure lashing at your feet
Dragging into the deep ocean of depression

The world is a beautiful place
    If you can see the light at the end of the tunnel

The world is a beautiful place
    If you can enjoy the time you have here and now.

Josh Hawkes (14)
Patcham House School, Brighton

The World Would Be A Beautiful Place If . . .

The world would be a beautiful place to be born into
If there were no terrorist attacks.

The world would be a beautiful place to be born into
If there were no bullies.

The world would be a beautiful place
If there were no wars.

The world would be a beautiful place
If there were no murders.

The world would be a beautiful place
If there were no fights or arguments.

The world is sunny and you're down
On the beach having an ice cream.

The world is a nice place when people are having a nice time
Laughing with their friends.

Edward Hartfield (14)
Patcham House School, Brighton

The World Is A Beautiful Place

The world is a beautiful place to be born into
If you like war always being so fun.
If you don't mind a lack of life some of the time
Just when everything is fine,
Because even in Hell they laugh all the time.

The world is a beautiful place to be born into
If you don't mind terrorism around.
Maybe some suicide bombers as well
Which isn't half-bad unless it is your home.

The world is a beautiful place to be born into
If you like seeing poverty everywhere you go.
Sometimes you see it on the streets,
People begging for money, only to be denied.

The world is a beautiful place to be born into
If you like tornadoes and hurricanes sweeping the nation.
Maybe even with a few earthquakes and tsunamis here and there.

The world is a beautiful place to be born into
If you don't care about HIV and AIDS.
It may even be better not to see a doctor as they can't save you.

The world is a beautiful place to be born into
If you don't value your life.
It is good if you don't die, but it will happen some day
As it does to everyone.

The world is the best place to be right now,
But in the middle of all that is *death,*
Waiting for you!
Waiting to catch you!
Waiting to torture you!
Waiting to kill you!

Jeremy Wakeham (15)
Patcham House School, Brighton

This Planet Earth

When you think of the Earth,
You think of plants and dirt,
Animals and people that lurk,
Water and streams and flowers bloom.
And you just think to yourself, what a wonderful world!
Indeed, it's a wonderful world!
You find people kissing,
People laughing,
People dancing,
And people loving.
And you still think to yourself, what a wonderful world!
Yeah, it's a wonderful world!
You see the sky is blue,
The clouds are white,
The grass is green,
And the sun is yellow!
But you definitely think to yourself, what a wonderful world!

Douglas Varney (15)
Patcham House School, Brighton

The World Would Be A Beautiful Place

If people did all think the same,
                And acted like it too.

If people never conflicted your reason,
                Just accepted it was true.

If no one disliked your personality,
                Or picked up your *ticks.*

If no one told you were wrong,
                Because . . .

The world would be a beautiful place,

If no one started acting *dumb,*
                Or told you to act your age.

If no one behaved maliciously,
                Or lived to carry out revenge.

If people were consumed by death.

Kiomi Maguire (15)
Patcham House School, Brighton

The World Is A Beautiful Place

The world can be a beautiful place to be born into
If you have your favourite flowers delivered weekly,
If your teacher doesn't stand over you tapping her feet impatiently.

The world can be a less beautiful place
If nobody ever listens to you
If you have no friends at your side when you are feeling sad,
When you say for *God's sake* at the person you're annoyed with.

The world could be a bit of a beautiful place
If there were less *chavs* and *townies,*
If there were more spiders and bats,
If there were more of the things *girlie-girls* hate.

The world could be a bit of an interesting place
If there were more mythical creatures,
If there were witches and wizards,
If there were half men/half beast creatures.

The world could be a scary place
If you could choose your death,
If you could be immortal,
If you could not worry about dying.

Rosie Nicholls (16)
Patcham House School, Brighton

The Giant

How tiny to a towering giant
Must these mighty things appear,
An ocean like a miniature puddle,
Its waves like metallic ripples,
A cathedral like an upturned needle,
A mountain like the lid of a bottle,
The tallest trees within the forest like a pen tip,
A jumbo jet, a toy plane,
A lake, a droplet of water,
And skyscrapers that touch the sky like
A chewing gum wrapper.

George Bounds (11)
Rydon Community College, Storrington

Sneagle The Black Beagle

I'm a black beagle.
My name is Sneagle.
My owner is a very bad boy,
And he treats me like a toy.
Instead of giving me hugs and pats,
He'll give me great big wallops and smacks.
He locks me in the house alone,
And never thinks to leave a bone.
One day I'm going to give him a fright,
I may even give him a bark or a bite.
One day when I break free,
I'm going to show him the real me.
That is the story of Sneagle,
The black beagle.

Sam Aviss (12)
Rydon Community College, Storrington

The Giant

An ocean like a tiny puddle
Its waves, shallow ripples
A cathedral like a Lego chapel
A mountain like a mound of mossy earth
The tallest trees within the forest
Like little twigs, hard to see
A jumbo jet, a colourful balloon
A lake a secret wishing well
And skyscrapers that touch the stars
As small as bungalows

Amy Louise Boxall (11)
Rydon Community College, Storrington

The Screams Inside Me

The key turning in the lock
I hear the screams inside me
But I stay still
Frozen with fear
But I still hear the screams inside me

He comes in and slams the door
And throws the keys at me
'Get to your room,' comes his roar
The screams are pushing, trying to get out

I begin to think, *why does he take it out on me?*
I sit all the time waiting for his orders
I hear the screams coming up my throat
As I hear his feet on the stairs

He comes in
My heart is racing, I feel all dizzy
The screams are dying off
As he comes over to my bed
I look into his eyes and I see he has a tear-stained face

His voice comes so soft, so quiet I don't hear
The screams are settling
'Sorry,' he repeats
I run over to him and give him a hug
For the first time
I feel loved.

But the screams are still inside me . . . hiding.

Amber Edmonds (12)
Rydon Community College, Storrington

My Poem

I was in my hutch, it was awful,
It smelt horrible, I felt really ill
My owners hadn't cleaned my hutch for ages.

I had no food or water
I was really hungry and thirsty
I really want to go outside and eat grass.

My fur felt really knotty
My nails hadn't been clipped for ages
They were like lions claws
I wish I had a nice hutch to sleep in.

Jessica Leask (11)
Rydon Community College, Storrington

The Giant

An ocean like a small pond.
It's waves like the ripple from a teardrop.
A cathedral like toy blocks.
A mountain like a pile of mud.
The tallest trees within the forest like a field of grass.
A jumbo jet as tiny as a baby's shoe.
A lake as small as a puddle.
And skyscrapers that touch the stars
Like a *Pepsi Max* bottle.

Nicole Davies (11)
Rydon Community College, Storrington

The Meaning Of Life

So what is the meaning of life?

Why are we here?

To live and to die
To do what we enjoy
To take care of each other
To create another generation of children
To have fun
To appreciate
To protect each other
To help each other
To love and to hate
To learn from our mistakes
To fall and learn to pick ourselves up
To take care of the environment
To learn about life
To protect our country
To protect the world
To explore
To tell the truth and a lie
To abide by rules and break them
To ask for forgiveness and to forgive.

Lewis Yearsley (12)
Rydon Community College, Storrington

Turn Back Time

I'm sure I can change
I'm sure I can
I'll be nicer to my teachers
I'll be nicer to my mates
I know I can

I'm sure I can change
I'm sure I can
I can help out
I can use good manners
I know I can

I'm sure I can change
I'm sure I can
I'll stop fighting and being rude
I'll behave in lessons
I know I can

I'm sure I can change
I'm sure I can
I don't want to be a bit of chewing gum
On the bottom of a shoe
I don't want to be scum
I'm sure I don't.

Jof Small (12)
Rydon Community College, Storrington

My Family

The baby likes to gurgle lots of different songs,
Brother Alan always gets his homework wrong.
Nan likes to sit listening to the blues,
Mum dances round and round in her bright green shoes.
Uncle Jim is being quiet, taking a well earned nap,
Grandad thinks he's a rapper, yo! and always wears a cap!

Chloe Gooding (12)
Rydon Community College, Storrington

If I Could Turn Back Time

If I could turn back time,
I would go back to when I got beaten by my father.
If I could turn back time,
I would go back to when my mum died, to get her back, alive.
If I could turn back time,
I would go back to when I got picked on at school.
I wish I could have done something about these things at the time.

Ashley Nicholson (12)
Rydon Community College, Storrington

If I Could Go Back

Why do we have wars?
All they do is kill innocent people,
And cause lots of sores.
The alarm of a ringing bell in a steeple.

They make little kids cry,
'Cause their mom has just told them,
Daddy go bye-bye,
Like a fox without a den.

A soldier gets shot,
He twists and falls,
He dies on the spot,
Floppy and droopy like a little rag doll.

If I could go back,
And change just one thing,
I would end wars like the one in Iraq.
And that might just solve something.

Thomas Rogers (12)
Rydon Community College, Storrington

Beyond The Stars

I remember my first boxer dog - KC
And my old neighbour Ron, in a way
These are memories of loved ones
Who have now, sadly, passed away.

I played cards with Ron
KC pulled me in my walker with rope
These are special memories
They will stay forever, I hope.

I also remember going on holiday
With my dog called Bonnie
Also Mum and Dad, two cousins
And my sisters, Caitlin and Hollie.

Memories of the holidays
Days on the beach in the sun
I remember going to my first school
Making new friends and meeting old ones.

Oh how I remember the good times, great memories!

Adam Cheesman (12)
Rydon Community College, Storrington

Great Memories

When I was two my dad won 2,000 pounds
When I got my MP3 I could listen to loud sounds
When I scored a hat-trick
I thought I should learn a new trick

When I learnt to drive
My sister was only five
When I got the Internet
I also wanted to get a pet

When my dad started banger racing
I wanted to go racing
When I got my first bike
I also got a trike.

Jack Strudwick (12)
Rydon Community College, Storrington

I Am A Tortoise

My name is Jeff, I am a tortoise
But a football to my owner
Just a tortoise to myself.
My owner feeds me once a fortnight
I need my food, I'm not alright.
I want to be with a family
Who care and live joyfully,
So I'm not pushed to the side
And forgotten in life.
I would like to walk around but can't,
This life is such a shame
I hope one day it'll change.

Howard Ayscough (12)
Rydon Community College, Storrington

The Abused Kitten

I'm small, lost, alone
I've run away
From my horrible abusing owners

My mum was covered in petrol
Then burned
My brother kicked to death
My sister's skull broken against a wall

Now there's only me
Scared
Unloved
Abused kitten
Please, come and save me.

Paige Matschy (12)
Rydon Community College, Storrington

If I Could Turn Back Time

The day I had that argument
The day he left our house
The day that he moved far away
I didn't even get a say.

The day that I was young
The day I could be free
The day that everything went OK
Not only just for me.

Sammie Chard (12)
Rydon Community College, Storrington

Away With Words

If I had a time machine
What would I go back to see?
Would I see the world begin?
Or would I see Lord Jesus?

If I could go forwards in time
What I'd see could change my mind
Would the world be run by robots?
Or would aliens destroy the world?

If I could see through someone else's eyes
Whose eyes would I look through?
Would I look through my friend's eyes,
To find out what they are like?

Ben Ireland (12)
Rydon Community College, Storrington

The Meaning Of Celebrity

What is the meaning of celebrity?
Is it the partying?
Staying out till midnight,
With journalists listening to your every word?

Or is it the fame and fortune?
Getting what you want?
The houses, the holidays, the special treatment?

What is the meaning of celebrity?
Is it the media?
Always being followed?
The rumours, fashion mistakes, people selling stories?

Or is it the work?
Acting, modelling, singing,
Bad movies, bad fashion, not top of the charts?

What is the meaning of celebrity?
The partying, the fame and fortune, the work or the media?
What is the meaning of celebrity?
I don't know, do you?

Alice Sleight (12)
Rydon Community College, Storrington

What's Happening?

What is a table?
What is a chair?
How can I read that table
Or style my hair?

For I don't know
What is out there.

People laugh at me,
They tease me,
For they won't let me be,
Even though I say please.

For I don't know,
Who is out there.

Where am I now?
I'm beginning to weep,
For I'm like a lost cow,
In a field of sheep.

I am blind,
I cannot see,
But I still don't mind,
For at least I'm me!

Charlie Reeves (12)
Rydon Community College, Storrington

If I Could Turn Back Time

If I could turn back time,
The sun would always shine,
And trees would grow so tall,
If I could turn back time.

If I could turn back the clock,
I would change all my bad memories,
People wouldn't die or get old,
If I could turn back time.

If I could reset time,
People wouldn't live out on the streets,
And remember bad experiences,
If I could turn back time.

If I could turn back time,
Homework wouldn't be set,
The summer holidays would be longer,
If I could turn back time.

If I could turn back time,
I would change the world,
That's what I'd do!
If I could turn back time.

Laura King (12)
Rydon Community College, Storrington

Puppy

The hand of my owner
Comes beating down on me
Sometimes I'm a complete loner
Then the kids come home and won't let me be.

I am a puppy, small and weak
With so much love to spare
Why do they make me feel like a freak
And then just stand and stare?

Dogs just bite their enemies
So why do you kick me?
So many bad memories
I just want to be set free.

I wag my tail
Sit at your feet
I fetch the mail
For that I get beat!

Callum Wyatt (12)
Rydon Community College, Storrington

Poor Little Pets

Every single day,
People come and pay,
For a lovely little pet,
Some owners are let,
To beat them up with a bat,
And they only get to eat rats.

Rebecca France (12)
Rydon Community College, Storrington

Imagination

From the tallest tree
To the smallest weed
Imagination rules the world

You could make pigs fly
Up into the clouds so high
Imagination rules the sky

You could make the softest leaf
Into a mastermind thief
Imagination rules the world

You could make a puddle clear
Into an ocean of fear
Imagination rules the sea

You could stop terrorists
If only imagination ruled the world

You are the only one who has the key
The key to let your imagination roam free.

Joshua Reeves (12)
Rydon Community College, Storrington

Stop The Bullies

Tumbling and falling;
Tripping and bawling,
Don't let them see me,
They'll take me back,
Back to the room,
Back for a smack, a pat on the back.

Once I was scared,
But now I'm not,
Once I was bullied,
But then it stopped.

Told a teacher once before,
Told them again, now they know more.
They did something about it as you can see,
The bullying has stopped and now I'm free.

Phillipa Scott (12)
Rydon Community College, Storrington

The Tiger

The tiger is wild and scary
The tiger's colour is orange and black
With sharp black stripes on its back.
It is big and scary and eats all the time.
But when it gets killed it is not cute or scary,
But lonely and dead and cold like snow on the ground.

Aimee Shepherd (12)
Rydon Community College, Storrington

If I Could Turn Back Time

If I could turn back time,
I would go back to when I was five,
I wouldn't go to school and I would skive.
I would sleep all day long,
And run around the house singing a song.
I would play with my toys, day and night,
And at the weekends I would fly a kite.
I would have fun playing with my friends,
And dream of driving a Mercedes Benz.

If I could turn back time,
I would go back to when I was two,
I would shout and scream,
And wouldn't worry about going to the loo,
I would crawl around without a care,
And wouldn't get the choice of what to wear.
I would laugh and cry
And would always lie.

Charlie Pollard   (13)
Rydon Community College, Storrington

If I Could Turn Back Time

If I could turn back time
I wouldn't be ninety-nine,
I'd rather be nine,
Playing with my toys and sharing what's mine.

I'd promise mum I wouldn't shout,
And stay and talk instead of storming out,
Be happy with what I've got,
Instead of getting cross about what I haven't got.

I'd be patient and not stamp my feet,
And try to be very sweet,
A nicer person you couldn't meet.

I'm sitting here, I am ninety-nine,
I've had a great time,
With lots of memories in my heart,
I have enjoyed everything from the start.

Emilie Metcalfe (12)
Rydon Community College, Storrington

The Rapping Rat

There's a rat down our street
He's really not normal,
'Cause the rapping rat is down our street
And he's really, really cool.

I've told my friends about him
They say I'm wrong
But I know the rat down our street
Is really, really cool.

Now everyone knows about him
I think he likes it
He is so with it
And he's really, really cool.

I saw him with his friends
He really played the fool,
'Cause there's a rat, a cat and a dog
And he's really, really cool.

Ben Hasler (10)
Rydon Community College, Storrington

Pony Dreams

I'm dreaming of Polos and peppermints,
Of hot days in the field.
Of long hacks,
Of buckets filled with pony nuts.

I'm dreaming of cuddles from my owner,
Of being groomed until I gleam,
Of being champion pony at the derby,
Of being a pony superstar!

Dreamer the Pony.

Emma Fulljames (10)
Rydon Community College, Storrington

The Cat

There was a cat
Who liked to eat rats

He didn't like dogs
Instead he liked frogs

He hated fleas
He got shaky knees

But one thing he loved from the family dish . . .
Was *fish!*

Josh Grantham (10)
Rydon Community College, Storrington

Snakes

Snakes slithering across the ground,
Slimy they are not,
Snakes slithering across the ground,
They can tie themselves in a knot.
Snakes slithering across the ground,
Lots of colourful patterns,
Snakes slithering across the ground,
Rough they really are,
That's snakes!

Jessica Streeter (10)
Rydon Community College, Storrington

The Jumping Course

Must keep galloping, must keep galloping,
Here comes the fence,
Let's jump!

Come on, keep going, come on, keep going,
Here comes a log,
Let's jump!

I'm done, I'm tired, I'm back in my field,
Warm in a cosy rug.
Lying down under midsummer sky,
Watching the world go slowly by,
I am the one colt who is satisfied,
With a win at the jumping course!

Hannah Bailey (10)
Rydon Community College, Storrington

Horse

Once I was a horse in a show
I galloped fast as I jumped the hedgerow
One day someone put a needle into me
It didn't feel all that little to me
I couldn't jump, I couldn't fly
I couldn't soar like an eagle in the sky
I spent many months stuck in a box
I couldn't go out and play with the fox
Every day someone brought me hay
And I greeted them with a little neigh
Now I'm mended and I can fly
I can soar like an eagle in the sky.

Joe Beer
Rydon Community College, Storrington

Cruelty To Dogs

A little black Labrador called Jess,
Lived in such an awful mess,
Her owner hit her with a stick,
And now she feels very sick,
She sleeps outside,
And her paws are tied,
She wants to escape one night,
To see a beautiful sight,
Her owner's very mean,
And he doesn't keep her clean,
She's managed to escape,
Someone found her by a lake,
She now has a family
And lives truly happily.

Michaela Groves (12)
Rydon Community College, Storrington

Through The Eye Of The Tiger

Crouching low in the prairie, hidden from sight
I wait silently to catch my prey
A passing gazelle is what I seek most
One that has strayed from the pack.

Then my prayers are answered
I see it coming closer and closer
Without knowing I'm here
I stalk it, never taking my eyes away.

Nothing can distract me now
The only thing I think of is my family
How we all need this gazelle
To save us from starvation.

In three, in two, in one . . .
I sprint for it, I run as fast as I can.
The gazelle gets tired after a while
'Til it finally gives up - my chance to pounce.

Scoring my long claws into its flesh
With a smile of success on my face
Then I drag it back, proudly, to my lair
Where I see my hungry cubs waiting!

Dominique Burton (11)
Rydon Community College, Storrington

The World

Smoke and fuel is everywhere,
Polluting me,
I can hardly breathe,
Gasping for air,
But it is getting worse,
Nobody cares for me anymore,
I ask for help but no one replies,
I am going to die.

The air is getting cleaner,
The sun is starting to shine,
I watch the birds swooping,
In the blue sky,
I am getting better,
I can finally breathe,
The people do care,
For the birds, trees and me.

Ellie Blunden (11)
Rydon Community College, Storrington

The Rabbit

I am a rabbit,
They feed me carrots and grass,
Leave me in a hutch,
To watch rain pour down on the house made of glass,
Maybe a bunch of grapes would be nice,
Or am I not really a rabbit?
Only a field mouse.

But perhaps a bit of advice,
Take care of this little mice,
I might cry -
Or am I a fly?

Actually this problem is a piece of pie,
No more am I a mouse or a fly,
I guess -
I am -
A rabbit!

Oliver Prior (11)
Rydon Community College, Storrington

Looking At The World Through
Someone Else's Eyes

Again, hit by my own father
Betrayed, his mates hit me again because they thinks it's funny
Under his watch all the time, he's making sure I don't tell anyone
Sacred, the few hours at school, I am here and can have fun
End of school, back home,
Hit this time for not cleaning the house in time
Death becoming closer, as he comes towards me with an empty
beer glass.

Max Johnstone (12)
Rydon Community College, Storrington

Bullying

People all around me
Calling each other names
But when the teacher comes in
She is so ashamed.

It makes me sad
When on TV
Animals kill other animals
For them to eat.

Sophie Rance (11)
Rydon Community College, Storrington

The World Through Their Eyes

My dad's away on a business trip,
Mum's at home, probably chewing her lip,
As I walk through the door I know something's wrong,
And that my sister has been in that nappy way too long.

I notice that Mum's got a bruise across her cheek,
They usually last about a week,
It doesn't take me too long,
To guess where this one has come from.

It's the day after Dad got home,
He was selling a flat somewhere in Rome,
His temper hasn't flared up yet,
But it won't be long I bet.

A cold, raw hand grips my heart,
As his hand whips her face, as fast as a dart,
Next he raises his fist on me,
Then brings down hard and buckles my knees.

Emma Watson-Jones (12)
Rydon Community College, Storrington

Squirrels

I woke up in the morning
And I ran out yawning.
I skittered down the trees
My eyes ran across the leaves.
Where was an acorn
To give to my friend Lorny?
And then I saw one in the road,
I ran across to put it with my load
But only then did I see
That there was a car coming at me.
I landed to one side
But sadly I had died.

Daniel Abel (11)
Rydon Community College, Storrington

Hannah

There was a girl called Hannah
She was alone for two days with a spanner to protect herself.
Her dad came back drunk and smacked her,
She ran to her room and called her best friend Jenni,
Jenni said not to worry.

Jenni was her friend her only friend ever.
She was alone again for seven hours
Her dad came back and smacked her again.
This time was worse, she stopped talking.
She only talked to herself and to her good friend Jenni.

She went to school,
She hated it just as much as being at home.
She got bullied.
She had a horrible name, she was called Loner.
She was so sad.
She tried to ring Childline but her dad wouldn't let her.

Jodie Burch (11)
Rydon Community College, Storrington

The Giant

How tiny to a towering giant
Must mighty things appear
An ocean like a puddle
A wave like a ripple
A cathedral like a Lego house
A mountain like some ice cream
The tallest trees like broccoli
A jumbo jet like a little toy
A lake like a speck of rain
And skyscrapers that touch the sky
Like shoe boxes.

Jonathan Harris (11)
Rydon Community College, Storrington

The World Through Someone Else's Eyes

My name is Frank, I'm a horse.
I live on a farm. I'm enjoying myself,
I like to run around the farm all day.
When I feel hungry I can eat as much nice green grass as I like.
When I feel tired I can have a rest for as long as I want.
As I grow up I'm getting strong.
I have to carry people,
That's not difficult.
But my old owner has gone,
His son is the leader of the farm.
He doesn't care about us.
I have to do much more work,
I have to carry more people.
I've got a bit in my mouth,
A heavy collar on my neck.
Next there was a saddle,
They made the nearing rein very tight.
When I want to go up the hill,
It makes me feel hurt.
But my groom doesn't care,
He hits me with a whip.
I'm getting very tired every time when I work,
I don't have much food,
Nobody to clean my home,
I'm getting weaker every day,
But I still have to work.
It's so unfair, people never care about animals
That are working for them.
Is there anybody kind who can help us?

Frank Howell (12)
Rydon Community College, Storrington

The Eagle

I am the eagle flying through the hot blazing sun, looking for prey.
I can see everything,
All the time I'm constantly looking for prey,
Ready with my sharp, white claws.
I swoop down.

Rabbit, mouse or rat, who should I feast on tonight?
Hare tonight, the chicks will be pleased.
I need to hurry before night-time ends,
Or the hunters will get me as a trophy.

Jacob Brown (12)
Rydon Community College, Storrington

Golden Eagle

A graceful stalker
Watches his peasants
Full of merciless glory
And humble power.

His glorious greatness
And his feathers of fire,
Look great as he wallows in his golden robe,
But not so much as he begins his royal massacre.

A regal arrow,
The airborne 'hitman'
With eyes of lightning
And a shadow of death.

Teeth of steel,
A proud hunter,
A majestic killer, thirsty for blood.

All flee his presence.
He is the golden warrior,
The emperor of the sky.

Jamie Curtis (10)
Rydon Community College, Storrington

The Golden Eagle

The golden, glistening king,
The royal hunter of the sky,
The one who knows when to attack,
The one who knows why.

He has a huge wingspan,
With golden glistening feathers,
A golden sparkling crown,
And if he's angry he could have a golden frown.

Whilst gliding through the clear blue sky,
The hunter finds his prey,
He feels hungry, starving and empty inside,
What chance does that poor bird have?

Innocent, young, defenceless prey,
Killed by a deadly, famished golden eagle.

Millie Charman (10)
Rydon Community College, Storrington

Barn Owl

Murdering vampire,
Deadly squawk,
The barn owl creeps,
So silent for war.

Swooping through the forest,
Like a bolt of fury,
Sharp, strong claws,
Getting mice, furry.

Powerful hunter,
In the black of night,
Diving and gliding,
Making all full of fear and fright.

Darting through the trees,
Ripping prey to shreds,
Are the things the barn owl likes,
Instead of sitting in bed.

Dark evil eyes,
Full of mischief,
Ready to kill.
The barn owl did it!

Oliver Seal (11)
Rydon Community College, Storrington

Grey Heron

Skulking bird.
Robe of water.
Sleek white wings
Which shine upon the river bend.

Hunting.
Hour upon hour.
Aerodynamic swimmer.
He has a beautiful shimmer.
Stalking his prey,
At the end of the day!

Early he rises,
Through the morning mist,
To have his morning drink.
Out of the corner of his eye,
He sees his breakfast . . .
And now the chase is on!

Tamara McLeod (10)
Rydon Community College, Storrington

The Barn Owl

The wise wizard is back in his lair
From a long bloodthirsty hunt.

He is the ghost of the forest
Stalking in the moonlit sky.
He is the death shadow of the air.

The wizard's beady eye
Catching a slick but slow vole.
He is as fast as a jet
Nose-diving at his delicious prey.

The dew is rising.
The sun is falling into valleys below,
Glistening as it goes.
While the hunter takes flight.

When the moon rises
The wizard wants to meet her shining face.

Clara Bunyan-Hird (10)
Rydon Community College, Storrington

Golden Eagle

The eagle soars through the air
Catching the raindrops as they fall from the sky.

Down, at the speed of light, swoops the king,
Choosing which slave to kill first.
Its piercing talons digging into the victim's flesh
And its beak rips the life out of the victim.

Golden crown upon his head, he is the ruler of the sky,
Wings so bright, menacing blood-red eyes.

David Morton (10)
Rydon Community College, Storrington

Barn Owl

A ghostly figure stalks the night.
Death is knocking on your door.
Snow-white feathers and a heart-shaped face,
It swoops down like a bolt from the blue.
Its piercing talons wreak havoc all night long.
He glows in the moonlit sky.
Tearing innocent victims to pieces.
Silently moving through the murky depths of the swamp,
A death shadow haunts you.

Megan Kimber (10)
Rydon Community College, Storrington

Golden Eagle

The ruler of the sky,
Whom he chooses will die.
Majestic hunter,
A regal champion with his glossy robe of feathers.
An imperial pilot
With his feathered crown.

He soars over the mountains high
And sweeps through the valleys low
He scans the land for innocent prey
And when he finds it he rips, tears and kills.
He switches to his combat stance,
They have no chance . . .
For he is the golden eagle.

Morgan Blake (10)
Rydon Community College, Storrington

The Meaning Of Life

What is the meaning of life, why are we here?
Do we really exist, why can't we fly like the birds?
Why is there a tomorrow getting so near?
How do you know voices really can be heard?

What's hot weather?
What's cold air?
Is life as light as a feather?
Is it something we can't bear?

What is love?
Is it our feelings inside?
Is it when we feel above,
Or is it something we can't hide?

When we live in the sky,
The clouds we can touch,
Time passes by and by,
Why does life contain so much?

Why do we cry?
Why are we here?
Why do we lie?
If someday we'll disappear!

Jade Holdaway (12)
Rydon Community College, Storrington

Leaving Good Friends

Leaving, goodbye friends,
I will never forget you,
We have been friends to the end,
Friends like you are few.

Ever since we met that day,
We played and played and laughed,
Sometime soon my friend we may,
Be playing again at last.

Having friends like you to know and love,
Helping me through my pathway of life,
Flying high like a soaring dove,
Clearing away my troubles and strife.

So, goodbye for now,
Au revoir, farewell, so long,
I don't know when or how,
But we'll meet again and we can sing our song.

Chloe Coward (12)
Rydon Community College, Storrington

Horrid Henry

Horrid Henry is so bad
He always jumps on top of Dad.
I wish he was always good,
Just like any other boy should.
Perfect Peter is always good,
But Horrid Henry never would.

Horrid Henry is so bad,
Mum is always going mad.
Horrid Henry has loads of baths,
As hot as a rocket blast.

What he hates most of all,
Is his brother, the stupid fool.
His favourite food is onion crisps,
But his worst is carrot sticks.

Monkeys live on top of trees,
But Horrid Henry eats the leaves.
Horrid Henry's coming home,
Yes, now it's time to make him moan.

Did I forget the homework too?
He rips it up and eats it too.
When Perfect Peter is alone,
He sits on him to break his bone.

His best friend is Rude Ralf,
The second rudest in the house.
At dinner time he always says,
'I'm full up, there's no room left',
But at dessert he stuffs his face,
And then he burps right in my face.

It's time to wash up.
Come on Henry, get cleaned up.
He comes back in with empty hands.
Ahh, you're just going completely mad!

James Collis (10)
Rydon Community College, Storrington

Rooney

I have a little pet,
He's so cute and so sweet,
I love him so dearly,
From his ears to his feet.

His name is Rooney,
He is furry and tiny,
His tail is stubby,
And his nose is so shiny.

He lives in my garage,
In a cage so cosy,
Each time I walk past him,
He pops out - he's so nosy.

He sleeps all the day,
He runs all the night,
He only likes darkness,
The light's far too bright.

He's always pleased to see me,
I love to hold him near,
He knows I'll bring him special treats,
And care for him so dear.

Thank you little hamster,
For being my true friend,
You really mean the world to me,
A friendship that'll never end.

Leiane Andrews (12)
Rydon Community College, Storrington

The Meaning Of Life

Life is like the weather, you never know what's going to happen next,
Life is like a bird, flying around,
Life is like water, on an endless journey,
Life is like the sun, always shining,
Life is like a busy city, never sleeping,
Time flies, but which way?
Backwards and forwards all day!

James Bush (12)
Rydon Community College, Storrington

Animal Rights

What is the meaning of life?
No one knows what it is.
I would be amazed if someone told me what it means.
But yet, why do we disobey the laws?
Or yet, why do we do savage things to animals?
For our amusement of pain?
Or maybe to reuse the main?

What is the meaning of life?
No one will ever know what it means.
Will anyone stand for animal rights,
Or are we just afraid?

Jack Hannah (12)
Rydon Community College, Storrington

Save Our Home

(Written in response to a piece of 'wild' land near my home which was under threat
I felt strongly that the animals etc should be left alone rather than even more
houses be built.)

Some people think we, animals, don't have a point of view,
Mainly the people who support the demolition crew,
What is better, stuffed full of wildlife or a noisy building site?
We have feelings too you know, we need you humans to support
our plight.

We, the birds, will have no homes if you come and destroy our trees.
So you builders, we beg you to leave our roosts, please.
We, the snakes, can't slither anymore because this is our only place,
If you silly men build houses here it will eliminate our precious space.
We, the mammals, will lose our dens and won't have any food,
In this complaint we are trying our best not to be rude.

Please think about the points and stop your plans,
And put nature in your own hands.

Will Steer (12)
Rydon Community College, Storrington

If I Could Turn Back Time

If I could turn back time
I would go back to when I was two
My mum always used to say, 'Get rid of that bad flu'
If I could turn back time
I would go back to when I was three
When I jumped off a rock and fell into the sea
If I could turn back time
I would go back to when I was four
When I got chased by a big wild boar
If I could turn back time
I would go back to when I was five
When I made a fool of myself dancing the jive
If I could turn back time
I would go back to when I was six
When I took too many sweets from the *pic 'n' mix*
If I could turn back time
I would go back to when I was eight
When there was a bully who thought I was his mate
If I could turn back time
If would go back to a few days ago to
When I started to write this poem.

Steven Mann (12)
Rydon Community College, Storrington

Barn Owl

A silent murderer,
A shadow in the night,
A ghostly figure, flying high.

A haunted beast from the misty sky,
Glistening feathers, soft and sensitive.

Huge beady eyes staring down at innocent prey,
Down he shoots like a cannonball.

Gliding over enormous fields,
Then waiting for night to fall.

Sharp piercing talons,
Digging into brown wood.

Moonlit sky,
They fly tonight.
Hazel bird with snowy white wings,
A silhouette that flew away.

Emma Pegler (10)
Rydon Community College, Storrington

A Slave's Days

Life has not been easy,
Born to be a slave,
I've never felt much happiness,
Except in my baby days.

I started to work when I was four,
An average age to start,
And my work is my life's core,
Until the world goes dark.

I am beaten if I do wrong,
I never seem to do it right,
When my master hits the gong,
I get a terrible fright.

I have no family to comfort me,
They were all sold on,
I have no friends, so you see,
My life has already gone.

Hannah O'Connor (13)
St Philip Howard Catholic High School, Barnham

Through The Eyes Of The Guitar

Its strings were lazily strewn across the floor,
Its neck bent up double,
As it lay against the cold attic door,
It wondered what had caused the trouble.

Where were the fans? the guitar pondered,
Baying for more and more,
Cheering, encoring, every night,
Roses and pennies galore.

Oh how he missed the smell of tobacco,
Wafting through the strings,
The aroma of alcohol filling the stage,
The shine of ten-carat rings.

Where was his owner? the guitar thought,
Who plucked the strings with ease,
His sweet melodies filled the guitar,
He always seemed to please.

What happened to the road trips,
Travelling across the world,
Held with cold hands for all to see?

Did nobody love it anymore?
Was it only a tool?
But why, oh why, the guitar asked,
Was he left on this disused stool?

Henry Greenslade (13)
Uckfield Community Technology College, Uckfield

Away With Words

Away With Words is an African little boy, who had just been given
food and shelter for just one night.
Away With Words is a British lad whose Xbox 360 wasn't
immediately right.
Away With Words is an 18-year-old child equipped with weaponry
out on the frontline in Iraq.
Away With Words is an 18-year-old youth, rebelling because he's
not allowed to go to the park.
Away With Words is a nice friendly hand when someone's lonely
or afraid.
Away With Words is a horrible angry gang, pestering vulnerable kids
for their trade.
Away With Words is a handicapped princess, in her daddy's eyes,
learning to read.
Away With Words is unforgivable, misunderstood, souls relying on
drugs such as heroin or speed.
Away With Words is a joining of races peacefully walking
hand in hand.
Away With Words are mimicking fools; whose open-mindedness is so
miniscule nobody understands.

Away With Words are beautiful things of life that just maybe, even for
that second, precious to your heart.
Away With Words can be horrible selfishness that everyone should
stop, not start.

Tom Bedwell
Uckfield Community Technology College, Uckfield

The Night-Watcher Man's Autumn Dawn

He stands at the school gates,
Alone.
Only his own gruff whistle to keep him company,
The 6.35am air, bitter and wintry.
As he watches the pale, golden sun
Rise up so weary and antique like.
The man living in fear of the chattering mass that pours in at 8.30am,
When he becomes so intimidated,
By the thing he defends each shadowy night.
The playground is bare,
The trees poised and stout,
Their leaves curled with the madness of summer.
The buildings and classrooms
Just simply 'there'.
This friendless authority
Left to go about his solitary business.
But soon,
With a jingle of keys and a rustle of a jacket,
He is gone.
The giggling, shouting mass of children soon to come thundering in
his wake.

Rachel Pavey (13)
Uckfield Community Technology College, Uckfield

Tick-Tock Clock

You may think I'm nosy
But what else is there to do?
I'm just a clock on the school wall.

This could be really boring,
Just going tick-tock, tick-tock
Then moving a hand around my face.

But life becomes much more fun
When the hurly-burly kids
Start rushing down the corridors.

They drop their books, shout and cry,
They trip over friends and sigh,
And teachers add to the melee.

'Stop running,' I hear them scream,
'Come here, get to my office!
You will spend your break time with me!'

But what I delight in most,
Shh, are secrets overheard
In quiet times during classes.

All I need are batteries
To keep my workings going,
With time changes now I am set.

Tick-tock, tick-tock, tick-tock, shh,
Tick-tock, shh, I'm watching you,
Tick-tock, tick-tock, tick-tock, tick-tock.

Eleanor Watson
Uckfield Community Technology College, Uckfield

My Dog Ruby

Insect muncher
Bone cruncher
Forest lover
High jumper
Human liker
Bed stealer
Tripe hater
Toy breaker
Ball chaser
Sock pincher
Attention seeker
Treat eater
Blanket chewer
Tail wagger
Bird stalker
Face licker
Water drinker
English Pointer
Always hyper!

Emma Crowhurst (12)
Uckfield Community Technology College, Uckfield

Trick Or Treat

Here they all come walking down the dark street
They look so scary, each one I meet.
They run up the steps, and knock on the door
'Trick or treat,' and 'Please sir can we have more?'
They walk away with smiles on their faces
And off they go to many more places.
My house next! I'm the dentist of the street,
They won't get anything from me that's sweet,
So I drop a toothbrush into each sack.
I don't want their teeth decaying and black.
They look in their bags and they think it's a trick,
But I care! I don't want kids getting sick.
Sadly they don't understand my great plight,
They hide in the hedge and give me a fright.
Hallowe'en and I've tried to be caring.
My door's been egged . . . my fence needs repairing.

Kayla Martinez (12)
Uckfield Community Technology College, Uckfield

The Hide-And-Seek God

There are people,
Many people,
And they're searching,
They look,
They seek,
They call,
They have been forever,
And will probably never
Find what they're looking for.
All of the people
Are split in agreement
To what they are trying
To find.
And to many a person,
This huge controversion
Is too big,
And boggles the mind.

Some people look at the shadows
That are cast upon the wall.
Some people gaze to the heavens
And through prayers they plead
And they call.
Some say
They're too busy to
Seek for religion
Within their personal pod,
And some
When you ask them,
Will certainly say that
The answer's a
Definite God.

We argue, we fight,
We kill and destroy,
We try to preach God's word,
But so many voices are
Shouting so loudly that
None of them
Can be heard.
The different beliefs and
The different religions can
Never be fairly true,
So harvest your knowledge
Respect all religions,
But base your beliefs
On you.

Maddie Broad (12)
Uckfield Community Technology College, Uckfield